T0064333

Be Strong

A Memoir of Bereavement

JOY EKWOMMADU

iUniverse LLC
Bloomington

BE STRONG
A MEMOIR OF BEREAVEMENT

iUniverse books may be ordered through booksellers or by contacting:

iUniverse LLC
1663 Liberty Drive
Bloomington, IN 47403
www.iuniverse.com
1-800-Authors (1-800-288-4677)

Because of the dynamic nature of the Internet, any web addresses or links contained in this book may have changed since publication and may no longer be valid. The views expressed in this work are solely those of the author and do not necessarily reflect the views of the publisher, and the publisher hereby disclaims any responsibility for them.

Any people depicted in stock imagery provided by Thinkstock are models, and such images are being used for illustrative purposes only. Certain stock imagery © Thinkstock.

ISBN: 978-1-4917-0901-6 (sc)
ISBN: 978-1-4917-0903-0 (hc)
ISBN: 978-1-4917-0902-3 (e)

Library of Congress Control Number: 2013917340

Printed in the United States of America.

iUniverse rev. date: 22 October 2013

This book is dedicated to my late husband, Marcellinus Chukwuemeka Ekwommadu. Emmy, as I fondly called you, you were the love of my life. I will forever cherish the brief but quality-filled life we shared together.

You will increase my greatness and comfort me again.

—Psalm 71:21 (ESV)

This book is dedicated ... my ... husband, Marcell ...

Mr Marcellinus Chukwuemeka Ekwommadu,
22 August 1972—21 October 2012

Contents

Contents

Preface

According to psychologist Abraham Maslow's famous hierarchy of needs, friendships and relationships are very important motivating factors in the quest to satisfy an individual's needs.

The sudden death of my husband, Marcellinus Chukwuemeka Ekwommadu, created a terrible void. As I struggled through my loneliness, the need to express my inner feelings grew very strong. Unfortunately, I had just moved to a new province where there were no family or friends around me. In my need to be heard, I started writing as a means of relieving my soul. As my written thoughts and words developed, the idea of putting them together into a book was born.

When I reflected on the last days of my husband, I felt that something was lacking in the way his life ended. Everything about his last days seemed to be rushed, beginning with his last trip to Nigeria. He rushed off to the airport, and we barely had time to spend with him there.

His funeral was planned in a hurry. Within a week of his death, his mother died as a result of heartbreak, so his family thought both funerals should take place on the same day. I feel that because of the double funeral, Emmy did not receive the kind of honour he deserved.

The funeral program that was distributed to guests was incomplete and inadequate. Normally, in Nigeria a funeral program provides the guests with important information about the person whose funeral it is. Contrary to this popular norm, nothing was mentioned in Emmy's program that could inform guests about the great man who passed so tragically. His biography was written in a rush, and many important details were missing. The most shocking part of the funeral program to me was the lack of a caption for the photo of Adaku, his beloved princess. People were left not knowing about one of his most treasured possessions.

So, I decided to write a book to accurately tell my husband's story to friends and well-wishers and also to provide a priceless keepsake for my children.

Be Strong: A Memoir of Bereavement is my attempt to capture the life of a rare kind of man whose ultimate goal in life was to satisfy his immediate and extended family. He worked hard to be a success so that his children could look up to him as a role model. This book will also help satisfy my innermost desire to do justice to the memory of my late husband. As friends and well-wishers read this book, I hope that they, too, will share in my experience and learn a lesson or two.

Acknowledgements

Thank God for his special grace in my life and the lives of my children. In every situation we find ourselves, the Bible says we have to give thanks to the Lord, so I thank God for keeping me and my kids safe and healthy through this rough period of our life.

My family is very thankful to Mr Henry Cole and his wonderful wife and son for all their support. The test of a true friendship comes when the going gets really tough. Akin, you are truly Marcel's best friend. May the good Lord grant you all your heart's desires.

I remain grateful to my family (both immediate and extended) for all the support I received when I travelled to Nigeria. Without their help it would have been almost impossible for me to move on. I especially thank my mother, Mrs F. N. Okoro, for her gentle loving kindness and for reminding me that all hope is not lost.

In a very special way, I wish to thank all the families in the Greater Toronto Area, Ontario, and the Orlu-Okiegwe Association of Ontario. Thank you all for coming out to support and pray with me and my children. Especially Mr Samuel Okafor; his wife, Ngozi Okafor; Mr Barthlomew Emedoh and his wife Gladis Emedoh; Mrs Elizabeth Siqueira and Mrs Sonita Krishnan, thank you for your love, kindness, and spiritual and emotional support. It means a lot to my family.

I wish to thank the staff and families of St Therese of the Child Jesus, Our Lady of Mt Carmel Secondary School, and the Knights of St Columbus. You showed me and my family what it truly means to belong to a community of faith. I remain eternally grateful to you for all your support.

I also wish to thank Mrs Becky Arogie and family, and Mrs Ihuarueze Agoha and family, for their never-ending support. A special thank-you to the African Catholic Community, Surrey British Columbia; and the families and staff of the Star of the Sea School who rallied around and supported me and my family. Now, I believe out of sight is truly not out of mind.

Finally, I am grateful to the godparents of my children: Mr and Mrs Teddy Ibekwe, Mr and Mrs Uche Dike, and Mr and Mrs Madumere for all your spiritual and emotional support. You have shown me you know the true meaning of your role in the lives of my children.

Introduction

One of the natural desires of man is to live a long, healthy life—to be there for all the milestones in the lives of his children and be ready to join his ancestors at an old age. No one is ever prepared for an untimely death, especially one that claims the life of a young, healthy, and vibrant man. It not only devastates the entire family, it leaves the immediate family questioning and wondering where they've gone wrong. It makes healing and moving on an almost impossible venture.

On 21 October, my husband, Marcellinus Chukwuemeka Ekwommadu, who had just turned forty on 22 August 2012, was involved in an accident far away from home that claimed his life. Afterwards, days rolled on into months, and I realized more than anything else that I missed my best friend.

Be Strong: A Memoir of Bereavement is about the struggles of a young family dealing with the traumatic effects of the loss of the most significant person in their life.

As my children grow up, I hope they never forget their wonderful father. By sharing this story in print, my ultimate hope is to give our children something to hold on to, to make a reference to, and hopefully be a substitute for their father's advice. They can read about him and think about what he would do in that situation.

This book is also for anyone dealing with grief who is looking for comfort. I hope they achieve that by reading about how my family is hanging on to our faith in God and taking it one day at a time.

I included Bible verses before each chapter; these verses have helped me when I needed spiritual guidance. I hope they will help and guide anyone who finds himself or herself in a similar situation.

I hope that the memory of my husband, Marcellinus Chukwuemeka Ekwommadu, lives on and is never forgotten.

My help comes from the Lord, who made heaven and earth.

—Psalm 121:2 (ESV)

Be Strong!

Be strong! I must have heard those words a thousand times after 24 October 2012, a day that I have officially declared can never be duplicated as long as I live. The day I learned about the death of my beloved husband, Emmy, he had travelled to Nigeria on a business trip on 16 September 2012 and was supposed to come back home to Canada to my children and me on 23 October. I spoke to him on the phone in the morning of 21 October; he couldn't wait to come back home. Unknown to me, that conversation was the last time I would hear from Emmy. After our phone conversation, he boarded one of the buses belonging to a company called ABC Transport, from Aba, Abia State of Nigeria, to Abuja, the central part and federal Capital Territory of Nigeria, where he would board his flight at the Abuja International Airport. Unknown to me, the bus was involved in a fatal accident and never made it to Abuja.

I tried to contact Emmy that night, to make sure he arrived in Abuja safely, but I couldn't get through. I figured I couldn't get through because in Nigeria, sometimes their cell phone network can be difficult to connect to. Thinking that all was well, and he would board his flight on 22 October, and arrive in Canada on 23 October, I did not have any cause to think otherwise, so I focused

1

on making his favorite soup, preparing for his return, and tackling the ever-so-busy life that comes with taking care of three children.

When my children and I went to pick Emmy up at the airport on the twenty-third and were informed he was a no-show from Abuja International Airport, I died a thousand times over. How could he be a no-show? If his flight was cancelled, why did he not inform me from Nigeria? I was convinced something terrible had happened. It was completely out of character for him not to inform me of a change in his travel plan or a delayed flight. It was at that point that I really started to worry. But never in my wildest imagination was I prepared for the news to come.

Be strong! Oh, those words—never a day passed after that without hearing those words. Friends and well-wishers all gathered around me, each with a similar tale they had heard from someone, had read somewhere, or had experienced.

When the news had first come, I sat on the floor, crying my eyes out and wishing that what I heard was a sick, cruel joke. But no matter how I wished for it, the reality was no joke. It was real, as real as night and day.

I was completely in a state of shock. How could this possibly be true? How would I tell my three kids about the news? How could this be happening? Was it really possible that my life, the way I had known it for the past twelve years, was over?

My mind kept wondering and questioning. All I heard were the words: *Be strong—you have to be strong.* Did I really want to hear them?

What did they mean by "be strong"? How was I supposed to be strong when Emmy was not with me? I always relied on him when the going got tough. How could I deal with this news?

As I reflect now on that horrible experience, I cannot help but revisit my past and what led to that day.

My Background

I am from Isi-Okporo Local Government Area in Imo State. I was born and raised in Lagos, Nigeria. My parents, Lt Barrister A. C. Okoro and Mrs F. N. Okoro, inculcated in me the importance of a good education and a sound moral and religious background. I remain thankful to them for their wisdom.

Growing up, I always pictured myself living somewhere away from Nigeria, preferably the United States of America or somewhere in the western part of Europe. At that time, I knew nothing about Canada, where I eventually ended up living. I wished to leave Nigeria, not because I did not like my family or the people around me or the country itself, but because I wanted to be in a country that had better prospects for me.

When I was growing up in Nigeria, I always felt different in my ways of reasoning when I compared myself to people around me. I have always had a strong sense of self. I never believed that anyone else held the keys to my freedom, the enjoyment of life, or my success.

I went to restaurants, movies, and places like the beach on my own without thinking twice about it. One time, I was having lunch on my own when my sister came in with a friend to eat, and she saw me eating by myself. She was amazed that I could feel comfortable there.

Her comment to me was, "How is it that you are OK eating here on your own?"

I told her I just felt like eating there, so I did. She looked at me with astonishment.

I guess God made me that way to prepare me for the ordeal to come later in my life.

In my university days, my friend and roommate, Ihuarueze Agoha, used to tell me a lot about life in the States. She was an American citizen, and I prayed earnestly for an opportunity to live the life of an American. The opportunity came when my big brother, then working in the United Kingdom, promised to take me to Canada if I did well in school. I read like my life depended on it, and after I graduated, I found myself in Canada on 4 September 1999.

In 2001, two years after I came to Toronto, I met a very wonderful man, Marcellinus Chukwuemeka Ekwommadu. How I met him is a story worth telling. On that fateful day, I went to a Nigerian grocery store, and there I met a young man, Chijioke, who spoke the same language as I spoke. After a brief salutation he noticed I spoke the exact same dialect as a friend of his living in British Columbia. He took my phone number and said he must give it to this friend of his to contact me. The next day, his friend (Emmy) called me, and we ended up speaking on the phone until my handset got so hot that we had to stop talking.

It turned out his dad fixed my dad's bicycle back in 1966 when Nigeria was involved in a civil war! I knew all his uncles personally. It was funny when, as our conversation progressed, he would mention the name of an uncle and I would say, "I know him!"

His dad was a good friend of my uncle, and four of my aunties were married in his village. It was a match made in heaven. Before we met physically, he called me on the phone daily, and anytime he called me, he was always in the kitchen cooking for himself.

I asked him if he ever ate out, and he replied, "No, I'd rather cook my own food, and besides, friends are always coming over to hang out with me. I'm known for my cooking."

I guess that should have been a hint to me that I would end up being in the kitchen a lot.

When Emmy was single, he loved to party, he loved to dance, and he was a free-spirited being. But he never got into any trouble with drinking, smoking, or any kind of trouble associated with recklessness.

When I asked him how he stayed so clear and focused in life, he responded, "I know who I am and where I come from."

I can still see the seriousness in his expression as he continued, "Being from a family where things are not just handed to you, I learned very early in life that success and failure lie in one's hands. If you work hard, pray, and never give up in times of trials and tribulation, you will definitely succeed in life. And if you always remember who you are and are determined that where you are from is not necessarily a determining factor of where you are going in life, you will be all right."

How I have held on to those words!

The first time we met was when he came down to Toronto to visit me. His smile captivated me, and I realized we were meant to be together.

In the first photo Emmy sent me, he had curls and a pierced ear. I remember looking at his photo and asking myself if he would be serious enough to commit to a relationship. When I was growing up, we believed that a man with curls and a pierced ear was just out to have as much fun as he could. However, "never judge a book by its cover" was a popular saying of my people, so I reserved judgment. Emmy turned out to be the very devoted type.

I visited Emmy in British Columbia before I decided to move there in order to be close to him. When Emmy took me to his apartment, I remember saying to myself, *What a clean guy!* His apartment was spotless. His kitchen was so organized, and he had everything in place because he was such a good cook. I took one look around his apartment and I said to myself, *Now, this is a guy worth being in a relationship with.*

The year after we met, I couldn't believe how much we had grown to love each other, so to celebrate our anniversary, we decided to share the reasons we fell in love. I told Emmy I fell for him because of his strong sense of responsibility and, of course, his good looks! He laughed and said he fell for me because of my strong sense of self and independence.

He used to say to me, "I am very happy that I met you, because I know you are a very capable and strong woman."

Now that I think of it, I wish he had not seen me as that capable. Maybe he would have stayed with me, because I am not strong enough to carry on without him.

In December 2002, we travelled to Nigeria to perform our traditional marriage rites, and on 19 July 2003, we were married at St Joseph Catholic Church in Port Moody. We both came from large families, but we had only a small ceremony then. However, on 4 December 2004, we had a grand ceremony in Nigeria, during which we renewed our vows in the presence of our families and friends.

Oh! What fond memories! The fondest memory I have of that day is when at the reception the band suddenly declared a dance competition between me and Emmy. Emmy brought out all his moves and danced and danced with the intention of winning. But when I danced, even the musicians had to apologize to Emmy for all his efforts, because there was no way he could win the competition. I still remember how his eyes dilated with so much laughter.

God blessed our union with Nnaemeka, our first son. I will never forget the pride and joy on Emmy's face the moment he held his first son in his arms. Fortunately, my honorary mom, Marguerite Wood, captured this moment with her camera. It was just a priceless moment.

Then came Chidube, our second son. Emmy was over the moon, and he kept bragging to his friends that he had the secret of making male children in the event they ever needed a lesson or two.

Five years after Chidube, we had our princess, Adaku. I cannot attempt to explain Emmy's mood when he held Adaku. He could not stop smiling.

Emmy called her Adaku, and he said she was the daughter of wealth. Wealth in my culture has little to do with physical cash but more to do with good things of life; it means having a family that loves you, health, and good friends. Her name simply meant she would be the daughter of all that is good; the daughter who would take care of him when he grew old; the daughter who would never forget her father's house; and the daughter who would be her daddy's best friend. This was the daughter whose wedding would be celebrated like that of a princess. Oh! I remember that day like it was yesterday.

Emmy referred to his sons as his soldiers. They were the boys who would never allow his name to be forgotten; the boys who would forever fight for their rights and the rights of their family; the boys who would definitely make him proud of being a daddy.

What a man! I guess a big part of the reason I am motivated to write this book is to let the world know what a man he was, and let his children know what a man they had for a father.

Mr Marcellinus Ekwommadu and wife, Mrs Joy
Ekwommadu, at their wedding ceremony, 19 July 2003

Mr Marcellinus Ekwommadu, and wife, Mrs Joy
Ekwommadu, at their vow renewal in Nigeria

Marcellinus Ekwommadu and Joy Okoro, later
Joy Ekwommadu, on their first date

Mr Marcellinus Ekwommadu, at the graduation
ceremony of his wife, Mrs Joy Ekwommadu

Mr Marcellinus Ekwommadu and wife, Mrs Joy Ekwommadu,
at the baptism of their son Nnaemeka Ekwommadu

Mr Marcellinus Ekwommadu and wife, Mrs Joy Ekwommadu,
at the baptism of their son Chidube Ekwommadu

Mr Marcellinus Ekwommadu and wife, Mrs Joy Ekwommadu, at the baptism of their daughter, Adaku Ekwommadu

The Ekwommadus and Joy's mother, Mrs Fidelia Okoro, at Adaku's baptism ceremony

Mr Marcellinus Ekwommadu at his first son Nnaemeka
Ekwommadu's first birthday celebration

Mr Marcellinus Ekwommadu at his second son
Chidube Ekwommadu's first birthday celebration

Mr Marcellinus Ekwommadu's princess, Adaku
Ekwommadu, on her first birthday

Adaku Ekwommadu's first birthday with friends and well-wishers

I wait for the Lord, my soul waits, and in his word I hope.

—Psalm 130:5 (ESV)

My Sweetheart

Emmy, short for Chukwuemeka, was a self-made man. He had a vision in life, which was to provide for his family and ensure that at all times we were OK and had all the basic essentials that life could offer.

He was born in Aba, on the eastern part of Nigeria. He used to tell me about how hard it was growing up. He had started supporting his family very early in life because of the difficult times his family had financially. His mother ran a restaurant, and his father was in the real-estate business. Emmy told me that, because his father was not very healthy, his career was not so stable, yet his father tried to be there for his family as much as he could.

Emmy said that when he was about ten years old, things were really rough on his family, so he had to help out by hawking goods. This affected his studies, because all that he could think of while other students were studying was what streets he should cover to try to sell off his goods. Emmy was very good at convincing people to buy his goods, even at that tender age, because he was a natural salesperson. There was little wonder he did so well in life through buying and selling.

He once shared an incident with me that I can't get out of my head. He said that back then his mother warned him never to accept

100-naira bills because there were a lot of fake 100-naira bills in circulation. I guess being a kid, although not just an ordinary kid but one determined to succeed, he forgot about the warning.

One day, he said, as he was hawking, a man called to him to buy some of Emmy's goods. Emmy said the man bought goods worth about 35 naira and handed him a 100-naira bill. Because on that particular day he made very few sales, he decided to accept the bill. But he had no change to give to the man. The man asked Emmy to go look for change while he watched Emmy's goods. Emmy said, being innocent, he left his goods with the man and ran off to look for change. By the time he got back, the man had taken the rest of his goods and disappeared, leaving Emmy with a fake 100-naira bill and an empty tray. Emmy said he cried much that day, but most of all, he learned never to trust strangers.

In Nigeria, when you decide to go into any trade, you have to be an apprentice under someone known as your "Oga," who is an established person in that trade. Because Emmy felt that going into business would accelerate his success and relieve his family from taking care of him, he decided to become an apprentice. Normally, it is understood between the apprentice and the Oga that after a set amount of years, the Oga would "settle" his apprentice (meaning, help the apprentice financially to establish his own business as a reward for his years of service). Emmy said that to his utmost disappointment, his Oga decided to kick him out just before his appointed time in order to avoid settling him.

Emmy said he was devastated, but his mother did all she could to raise the money he needed to start his business.

Because Emmy was eternally grateful to his mother for the sacrifice, he said the first thing he did when he started to achieve success in his business was to buy his mother a house. Emmy loved his mother so much, and his mother never took matters concerning him lightly.

Emmy demolished their family house in the Umuezeiyu village of Amauju-Isunjaba Town, in ISU Local Government Area, located in the eastern part of Nigeria, because he wasn't satisfied with the standard of the house. He built a beautiful bungalow for his parents and siblings so they would be comfortable when they travelled to the village. His family lived in the city of Aba, in Abia state; usually once a year, they visited the village for Christmas holiday, so they would need a place to stay. Then he built another house for me and our children in the same compound. He said he loved for us to stay in our own space when we travelled, but before he could do that, he had to make sure his siblings were comfortable too.

Sometimes I still find it difficult to believe how committed Emmy was to his siblings. He was the kind of brother everyone would wish for. I tell my kids to always be there for each other, because that is what family is truly for. Their dad set a wonderful example for them to follow.

In 1995, Emmy left Nigeria for Israel. When I asked Emmy why he decided to go to Israel, he said, "As the firstborn child, it was my duty to take care of my family."

Emmy said for him to properly take care of his own future and that of his family, he had to leave Nigeria. He did and worked really hard. Emmy said he was never comfortable until he came to Canada in 1998.

21

When Emmy arrived in Canada, he met a really nice couple, Veronica and Howard Allen. He said they were so nice to him and even helped him settle down in his first apartment. Emmy always believed in helping people, especially those who are new to the country. When I asked him why, he told me about how special he felt when Veronica and Howard helped him. He wanted to make others feel the same way too.

When I was in my teacher-education program, my workload seemed to be too much, and several times I almost gave up. But Emmy solidly stood by me.

He said, "It would be sad to give up your dream of becoming a teacher because quitters never win."

I still remember those words today, and I remain eternally thankful and grateful to God that in this lifetime I was blessed to meet a man like my Emmy—a man who would stand by you in difficult times.

When we were dating and I was still an international student here in Canada, I travelled to Nigeria without checking if my documents were in order. On my way back to Canada, in Britain, I was refused entry because, though my student authorization was valid, I had an expired visa. This was on a Friday. I called Emmy, sounding dejected and lost. His soothing voice on the phone calmed me down immediately. He called me every hour to make sure I was OK. Finally, Monday came, I renewed my visa, and I came home to the welcoming arms of my Emmy.

Emmy never joked with his brothers. His immediate younger brother, Nonye, told him that he would like to travel out of the country to buy the products that he sold in Nigeria. He told Emmy that he would make more profit if he travelled out of the country himself to buy his goods rather than buy from dealers in Nigeria. Emmy felt that this made sense because Nonye would be cutting out the middle man and in the process make more profit from his business. Emmy supported him both financially and morally.

Nonye travelled out of Nigeria to pursue his ambition in China, only to be stuck at the airport. He was nervous when he called Emmy on the phone. Emmy calmed him down and talked him through the whole situation. Emmy kept contacting him until he finally left the airport and flew back to Nigeria, where he is based now.

Emmy helped set up both his brothers, Nonye and Onyekachi, in business.

When Onyekachi, his younger brother, finished high school, Emmy insisted that he further his education and promised to fund it. Onyekachi said that going to college was not for him and that he would rather go into business.

Emmy assisted him financially in his international business venture. Onyekachi now travels to China to buy menswear in wholesale quantities and sells his goods in Ariara Market in Aba, Abia State.

Emmy believed that if his brothers were financially stable, the family would progress. I truly hope they never forget their brother and his efforts towards getting them to where they are today.

Part of Emmy's business in Nigeria was real estate. We have properties in Aba, Abia State, that are rented to tenants. Emmy was so kind to his brothers that, though he helped establish them in business, he let them stay in our property rent-free, so life would be a lot easier for them. That is how devoted he was as a big brother.

When Emmy's mom was very sick, Emmy brought her to Canada for medical treatment. Unfortunately, when she got here, her situation was really bad. She needed surgery in her hip, neck, and knee. And she had a bad cough that was a result of her cooking over wood fires for a long period of time when she had her restaurant business.

Doctors in Canada couldn't treat her because those she saw said Canadian health-care insurance would not cover her because she was a visitor. One of the doctors we saw recommended we take her to South Africa for treatment. Emmy left everything and flew his mother to South Africa. She got her surgeries, and her condition became manageable before the incident.

That is how seriously Emmy took his responsibilities concerning his family.

During one of my trips to Nigeria, Nonye, Emmy's brother, told me that one of the reasons he was successful in his business was because of Emmy's influence. He told me that because he lives in one of our buildings, his business colleagues often think that he must be quite creditworthy, so they never hesitate to give him goods on credit for him to sell, make profits on, and pay them back.

Emmy was a truly domesticated man. Every Saturday, he would clean to ensure that our home was spotless, because he wouldn't want to burden me with the extra responsibility of keeping a clean home since I did a good job of cooking and mothering the kids.

After our kids were born, when he came back from work, he picked them up and sang songs to them in our language until they fell asleep together. Emmy always fell asleep with them in his arms.

Emmy believed, more than anything else, in the importance of bringing up children in a God-fearing environment. He was very adamant that the children go to church every Sunday.

He used to say, "Bring them up the right way, teach them good virtues, and they will not depart from those when they grow up."

Emmy was a devout Catholic and an active member of St Matthew's Parish in Surrey, British Columbia.

The parish priest said that in our parish all ethnic groups had associations that fostered the needs of their people. He suggested that, if the Africans in our parish could come together and form an African Catholic Association, it would mean that we could have our own Mass and it would give our children an opportunity to learn our language and experience how the Mass was celebrated the African way.

Emmy was so excited about this that he completely engaged himself in the process of forming such a group. Emmy was the vice president of the association and did all he could to make sure that the African Catholic Association came to life. Emmy had never belonged to the choir, but when the association was allotted a spot every last Sunday of the month to celebrate Mass, Emmy joined the choir as his own way of ensuring the Mass ran smoothly.

Emmy was such a traditionalist that he believed that, no matter where he lived and where his children were born, they were still Nigerians. He went out of his way to teach his children Nigerian culture. He only spoke our language (Igbo) to them, because he strongly believed that if they heard and could speak their language, when they visited Nigeria or when we eventually moved back to

Nigeria, our children would blend in and not be strangers in their fatherland.

I remember him telling me what happened to him on one of his journeys back to Canada from Nigeria that illustrated the importance of speaking and understanding a different language. He said as he was passing through Nigerian immigration, the immigration officers assumed, based on his appearance and name, that he did not understand Hausa, which was the language spoken by inhabitants of the northern part of Nigeria. However, Emmy understood Hausa very well because he did a lot of business with the northerners and had picked up the language.

When these officers saw Emmy, they said in their language, "Look at this Omo Igbo [meaning Igbo man]. Let's look for a way to milk his dollars."

Emmy said he pretended he did not understand what they said. The officers asked him to open up his bag and asked him irrelevant questions so they would have an excuse to extract money from him.

Finally, my husband spoke in their language and said, "See, this Omo Igbo understands Hausa; I understood every word you said about me."

He said the officers were so shocked that they let him go immediately.

I am so happy he emphasized teaching our kids our language, because now when they travel to Nigeria, they understand everything people say—especially those things that people assume they will not understand. It's a good way of protecting themselves.

Having two boys close together in age can be physically challenging sometimes, so I am thankful for Emmy's energy. He was always there to take them to their various sporting activities. The church we went to had a basketball court, so on Saturdays during those beautiful summer days, he would take them to the court and they would have a game of basketball.

In life one should really cherish the little things, like spending time with your family. We tend to forget how important this is because of how fast-paced life in this part of the world can be. Life is not necessarily about buying the best house on the block or driving the best car or even buying the nicest toys or stuff for our children. It is always good to ensure that we spend quality time with loved ones. Because, when you look back someday and they are not there, you will only have the good memories you made together to hold on to.

Trust me!

Mr Marcellinus Ekwommadu and son Nnaemeka, after winning a bowling tournament

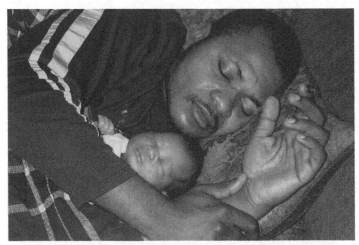

Mr Marcellinus Ekwommadu and son Nnaemeka enjoying a peaceful night's sleep

Mr Marcellinus Ekwommadu and son Nnaemeka Ekwommadu
having fun on the glass floor of the CN Tower

Mr Marcellinus Ekwommadu and son
Nnaemeka dancing at a friend's party

**Mr Marcellinus Ekwommadu, proud of being a
father when his son Nnaemeka was born**

**Mr Marcellinus Ekwommadu carrying
his son Chidube Ekwommadu**

Mr Marcellinus Ekwommadu and son
Chidube enjoying their sleep

Mr Marcellinus Ekwommadu and son Chidube, waiting
to be served at one of their father–son outings

Mr Marcellinus Ekwommadu and son Chidube having fun at the CN Tower, Toronto, Ontario

Chidube and Daddy having a blast

Mr Marcellinus Ekwommadu giving son Chidube a bowling lesson

Mr Marcellinus Ekwommadu and daughter bonding

Adaku Ekwommadu, making sure Daddy is fed

Mr Marcellinus Ekwommadu's princess Adaku
Ekwommadu in a Red Riding Hood costume

Mr Marcellinus Ekwommadu and daughter enjoying a peaceful night's sleep

Mr Marcellinus Ekwommadu, spending time with his daughter, Adaku Ekwommadu

Mr Marcellinus Ekwommadu and his
daughter on her second birthday

Mr Marcellinus Ekwommadu and his mother-in-law,
Mrs F. N. Okoro, and a dear friend, Mr Uche Okafor, at
the communion ceremony of Nnaemeka Ekwommadu

The Ekwommadus and their friend Mrs Tenneh Okafor at the
holy communion ceremony of Nnaemeka Ekwommadu

Mr Marcellinus Ekwommadu's second son Chidube
Ekwommadu on the day of his holy communion celebration

Mr and Mrs Henry Cole and their son, Mobolaji Cole, with the Ekwommadus at Chidube's holy communion ceremony

The Lord is your keeper; the Lord is your
shade on your right hand.

—*Psalm 121:5 (ESV)*

Hard Worker

From the moment I met Emmy, I knew he was a hard worker. He was a businessman and was very successful at what he did. Before he left Nigeria, he was a trader. His business involved a lot of travelling. He would travel from the northern part of Nigeria (Kano State) to the eastern part (Abia State). He felt that he could make more money doing business that way than working in an office.

After he travelled out of Nigeria in 1993, the following years of experience convinced him that he was meant to be his own boss. So, when he came to Canada in 1998, he opened up his own grocery store, Bamboo Smoke Shop, in Surrey, British Columbia. He also did a lot of shipping of cars and goods to Nigeria.

His ultimate goal was for us to relocate back to Nigeria, where he would build his own hotel. I would build and run my own school using my experience from Canada, and we would have our own businesses and retire early. We would work hard now and have all the fun later. That was the plan, and he worked towards it with determination that it must become a reality.

In March 2011, Emmy went to Nigeria and acquired a piece of land in the Federal Capital Territory of Nigeria, Abuja, where he would start building his dream hotel. He named it Majoy International Hotel, a combination of our names, Marcel and Joy.

He had an architect design the hotel. He was on top of the world, and finally he was on his way towards achieving his biggest dream.

In January 2012, we started to look into moving to Toronto. At this point in our lives we no longer felt as attached to Vancouver as we had previously. We had just sold our business, and I was working on call in various Catholic schools as a substitute teacher. The only thing that really kept us there was the wonderful school my children attended.

Emmy's shipping business was really doing well, and he travelled often to Ontario to buy his goods and cars to ship to Nigeria. In the spring of 2012, we decided to take the kids on a little vacation to Toronto and get a feel for what the whole family thought of it.

The kids fell in love with the city after visiting the CN Tower and Niagara Falls. However, it wasn't easy for them to think of leaving their friends and lives as they had known them. Change can be very hard on children—they are natural creatures of routine.

I had lived in Toronto when I first came to Canada, and I really liked the idea of moving there again. In August 2012 we made the big move. We relocated from Vancouver, British Columbia, to Mississauga, Ontario. We felt there was no better time than the present.

Though it was stressful in some ways, we felt really happy with our decision. Truth be told, we never felt happier in our marriage than we did the few weeks we spent together in Ontario. We were able to get a place in the area where we wanted our children to go to school, and travelling to Nigeria was a lot cheaper from Ontario compared to travelling from Vancouver. Life in general was a lot more affordable for us, and we were truly in a happy place.

About six weeks after we moved to Ontario, on 16 September 2012, Emmy travelled to Nigeria on yet another business trip. This time I wasn't very happy with his travel, because we had just moved to this new city, where I barely knew anyone, nor did I have a job. I felt it would be nice to take it slower and adjust to the new city. But Emmy convinced me that he had to make that trip.

Looking back, I now question where the feelings of discomfort surrounding this particular trip came from. Did my subconscious self sense that something bad was going to happen? I remember about a week before he travelled, before we went to bed I told Emmy that suddenly I wasn't very big on the whole idea of us returning to Nigeria. I suggested that instead we should invest everything we had in Canada. But he said because he was the first son of his family, he could not live outside our home country and he had to ensure that our kids were familiar with Nigeria. His dream was for us all to live happily in Nigeria.

We were in a rush on the day I took him to the airport. He was supposed to board the late-afternoon flight, so we quickly picked the kids up from school and rushed off to the airport. We barely had time to sit with him before his flight because he was running so late, so we dropped him off and said a very quick goodbye.

His last words to us as he went through the doors of the airport were, "See you all soon—love you."

If anyone had told me as we drove off that it was the last time I would ever set my eyes on the love of my life, I would never in a million years have believed it.

I now keep asking myself over and over again, *Why did I let him take that trip? Why didn't something happen on the way to the airport to disrupt his entire trip? Why did he not fall down our flight of stairs on our way to the airport? At least he would be alive with a broken leg.*

He travelled around a lot while he was in Nigeria, trying to get our hotel started. He shuttled from Aba in the eastern part of Nigeria to Abuja in the central part. Emmy was scheduled to leave Nigeria on 16 October, but he called me on the twelfth and told me he would postpone his return until 22 October.

I was not happy, because at that point I was really tired of taking care of the family by myself. I agreed after he pleaded that he had to postpone his return to enable him to tie up loose ends. I really had no choice. I look back now, and I ask myself, *Should I have done more to make him stick to his original return date? If he had stuck to his original return date, would this have happened? Why didn't something happen to prevent the change of plans? Why did I not pretend that I was sick and unable to function so he would have stopped whatever he was doing and come home alive? Why? Why? Why?*

The dream that never came true. Proposed hotel
in Abuja, Majoy International Hotel

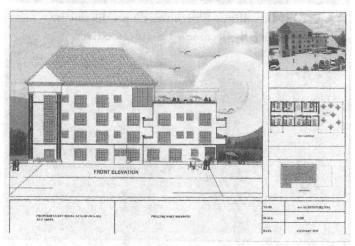

Front elevation of Majoy International Hotel

Mr Marcellinus Ekwommadu on the day he
officially became a Canadian citizen

Mr Marcellinus Ekwommadu closing up Bamboo Smoke Shop

Mr Marcellinus Ekwommadu performing at the cultural day
celebration at St Matthew's RC Parish, Surrey, British Columbia

Mr Marcellinus Ekwommadu enjoying an
African dish on one of his trips to Nigeria

Chief Cornelius Ekwommadu,
Mr Marcellinus Ekwommadu's father

Mrs Racheal Ekwommadu,
Mr Marcellinus Ekwommadu's mother

Mr Marcellinus Ekwommadu with his honorary
mom and dad, Mr and Mrs Wood

Mr Marcellinus Ekwommadu and his sons, Nnaemeka and
Chidube, at the Amauju Okorosha Festival in December 2009

**Mr Marcellinus Ekwommadu and his family
visiting the Niagara Falls in Ontario**

The Ekwommadu family at CN Tower, in Toronto, Ontario

Mr Marcellinus Ekwommadu and his family at the wedding
ceremony of dear friend Mr Morgan Ikedum and Pamela Reynolds

Father of the fatherless and protector of
widows is God in his holy habitation.

—*Psalm* 68:5 (ESV)

Horrific Day

On 23 October, the day of his planned return, I was supposed to pick Emmy up from the airport. I got the kids from school, and we were so excited. The kids were dancing around, and they had so much to tell their father, especially about their new school and their new friends. I was all tingly—it felt like an eternity since I'd seen him. I just wanted to hold him. I made him his favourite soup (bitter leaf soup), just like I used to when he travelled.

When I got to the airport, he wasn't there. I called his cell phone, but he did not pick it up. I then checked with the airline only to be told that he had not shown up to board his flight from Abuja. That was when I started to panic.

I called Nigeria, but no one answered the phone. I felt it was really out of character that he would miss his flight and not inform me. I kept calling his brothers and my sister who lived in the same area as my brothers-in-law, and I kept texting everyone, yet there was no response.

At this point I was a walking zombie. I did not know what to think, except that something very bad had happened. That night, I couldn't sleep, and I kept phoning and trying to hear something, anything at that point, to keep me from losing my mind.

I finally got my sister on the line, and she told me that my husband had been in a bus accident and that he was in a coma. Of course, he couldn't speak to me on the phone.

I panicked, but at least there was hope—he wasn't dead. All I would think of was how to get to Nigeria and bring him back to Canada for treatment. So I started calling the insurance company to start arranging for that.

Morning came, and a friend of mine and her husband who had been helping me with trying to contact Nigeria knocked at my door around 5.30 a.m. They insisted on taking me and my children to their place that morning, because they did not like how stressed I looked. I explained the situation to them, and they said it was a good thing we had insurance to help me out.

They started calling the few people we knew in Vancouver to inform them of the situation. My friend prepared my boys and took them to school, and she and her husband drove me back home. A handful of people who I knew started arriving at my place. I thought they were there because they had heard of the accident.

Then, my friend's husband told me that my husband had died.

My whole world crumbled before me. My brain froze. I turned to him, and I remember saying it was a lie, but he kept saying it over and over again so the news would sink in. Oh, that day!

After I got the horrible news, I remember crying so much that I felt like I was going into shock. I was also very angry that this should be my fate.

I asked myself and God many questions. Why should this happen? Why should he be one of only two people who died out of the seventeen who had been on the bus? Why did I not insist that he abandon his unfinished business and come back home like he originally planned? Why did I even let him travel, when we had only just moved to a new city? Why hadn't something happened to prevent him from taking that bus? Why didn't God prevent him from taking that bus? Why?

After I was able to gather myself together emotionally, I called my boys and broke the news to them. How I was able to do it remains a mystery to me to this day. My boys, seven and eight years old then, cried hard, but I found it in me to hold them close and let them cry it out.

As if the tragedy of losing my Emmy was not enough, another death lurked around the corner. Four days after my husband's death, his mom, who had been in very frail health, could not bear the loss of her first son, and her poor heart gave in to the tragedy of the loss.

So, there I was not only mourning the death of my husband, but I was also mourning the death of a dearly beloved mother-in-law. I was dealing with the loss of two members of my family in a country where I had no relatives to help me with the grieving process, *not one!* That was the hardest part.

Then came another round of questioning: *Why me? Did I do something wrong? This is just too much for one person to handle. Why not one at a time? Who do I mourn? Has this type of ordeal ever befallen a single person?* The questions were endless.

I have since realized, after many days, weeks, and months have passed, that the greatest lesson I have learned is to try to let go of the questions and put my hope, faith, and trust in the Lord. Once I did that, I started my long journey towards the healing process.

The Lord is near to the brokenhearted
and saves the crushed in spirit.

—*Psalm 34:18 (ESV)*

Life after the News

I guess the hardest part of this ordeal was the suddenness of it. Maybe if I'd had a little time to prepare for it, it wouldn't have seemed so unreal.

I had buried my father barely a year before. In the case of his death, the family had time to prepare for it. He was sick for about ten years. He battled with his prostate, although it wasn't cancerous, and he was diabetic. In his last years on earth, he was really tired of his medications and wished to "rest". He looked very frail and weak the last time I saw him, and I remember him telling us exactly what he wanted his funeral to be like, so we were prepared.

I know I can't compare both situations. Emmy was so young. I guess my point is, if I had seen him before he passed on, it would have made it a tiny bit easier to understand the situation. Maybe he would have said something to me or to our children—something that we could hold on to. Or I might have been able to hold his hands while he made the transition.

The thought of his last moment on earth will forever trouble me. I keep thinking, *Was his last hour very painful? Was he aware that he was going to die? Did his life flash before him? Did he simply slip to unconsciousness and gradually give in?*

I hope every day, when these thoughts come to me, that he did not suffer at all. These are the thoughts that have haunted me ever since the incident occurred. The thought that he died away from home with no family member with him, just strangers and a horrible fate, makes it unbearable.

Emmy was a perfectly healthy man who went to the gym three times a week. Five years ago he started visiting our family doctor once a year to make sure all was well with him. In fact, if his death could have been prevented by sheer physical strength, he would definitely be alive today.

After I heard the news and before I went to the funeral, I still kept calling his Nigerian number, because deep down, I wanted to believe that I was having a horrible nightmare. I wanted Emmy to pick up the phone and tell me it had all been a dream and we would go on with our lives and our plans. But that never happened.

Being alone and new in this city, I had to run little errands, like getting our papers ready for travel, getting myself and the children immunized, getting our plane tickets, etc. I had to drive myself, and I remember one time when I was driving, I got so emotional that I had to stop my car in the nearest space I could find and just let the tears run. I also remember driving past my house several times because I was so deep in thought. On more than one occasion, I drove into my neighbor's driveway, went to their door, and tried to open it with my key. Thankfully, my key did not open their door, and I realized I was in the wrong house!

Sometimes, I get so frustrated because I should have had a little time to myself to grieve. I felt with all the responsibility of taking care of three children and preparing for the funeral, I had no time to really check into myself and mourn without the distraction. Sometimes the distraction could be a good thing, but I just felt I needed to be completely alone to really process the loss of my husband.

As our departure date drew nearer, I was in serious conflict with myself. How was I ever going to be able to see Emmy lying there without moving? If I saw him lying there, lifeless, that would mean it was really true and he was never coming back. On the other hand, even though it would be bitter, it was the only way to really face the reality that Emmy was truly gone. It would be the first step towards healing my heart and my soul.

As I prepared myself, I kept hearing those words from friends and well-wishers: "Be strong. You have to be strong for the kids."

The other phrase I heard so often was, "Be strong. It is an abomination to be lost yourself, when you just lost your husband."

Did I really have any choice but to be strong? I didn't think so, even though I was tempted a lot of times to scream, "I don't want to be strong! I just want my darling husband back!"

Gradually, I turned my attention and focus towards God and completely put my trust and hope in him. I told him that, though I was afraid of embarking on the journey to Nigeria, I owed it to myself and my husband to make the trip. Through prayers with friends and well-wishers, I was able to build my spiritual self to make the journey to Nigeria. I guess at this point my personality kicked in, and I decided to be there for my family and do what needed to done.

You who have made me see many troubles and calamities will revive me again; from the depths of the earth you will bring me up again

—*Psalm 71:20 (ESV)*

Trip to Nigeria

Family is truly very important. I would not have survived the days preceding the funeral, the day of the funeral, and the days after the funeral without my family. When I arrived in Nigeria, I went to my family in the city of Umuahia. My family surrounded me with so much love and support. They completely took over my life, and they shared my grief.

Most of all, because I was home around family, I had a little bit of time to process the disaster that I was living. They offered different kinds of support, ranging from just being there with me and listening to all my fears, worries, and concerns, to offering practical help.

The greatest help I received from my journey was before the funeral when my eldest sister, Mrs Margaret Torty, organized a group of widows to talk to me and share their experiences. Some of them were widowed much younger than I was, and they had pretty rough lives after the deaths of their husbands. After hearing their stories, I began to feel less horrible about my situation but actually felt sorry for some of them. I also met some who, after the loss of their husbands, went on to become so successful that nobody would guess they ever went through the ordeal. That gave me hope. Again, the meeting ended with lots of "Be strong. The Lord is your strength."

The next step was to travel to my husband's village, Umuezeiyu, in Amauju-Isunjaba Town, ISU Local Government Area. I didn't look forward to that, not because I did not want to pay my last respects to my husband, but because I did not know what fate awaited me. In the history of my people (the Igbos), widows have often been treated so badly that you wonder how people could be so cruel.

They make widows do unspeakable things, like forcing them to cry publicly in the early hours of the morning. Even if these poor widows do not want to, they are forced to cry publicly or else they are falsely accused. The villagers want them to shout at the tops of their voices so people know they are mourning. Widows are asked to sit on the bare floor and cry with all visitors who come to pay their condolences. Widows have to show physical depression because they have lost their husbands. The villagers say it's part of tradition, but sometimes it really depends on who is enforcing the tradition.

I arrived at the village with a busload of family members and prayer warriors (people whose job is to assist you and your family in praying earnestly). As I entered our gate, my legs gave way, and I almost fell down to the ground. The prayer warriors caught me. They prayed with me and explained that it was to be expected. Looking back, I think I was overwhelmed by the feeling that I was in the place where Emmy was born and the place where he would be laid to rest.

I felt so alone, even though I was with many people. This was a place where I always went with Emmy, and I didn't remember spending time there without him, so the realization of the situation almost knocked me down.

That night, the prayer warriors had a night vigil with me. We prayed for my strength, my wisdom, and the soul of my Emmy.

We prayed for everyone coming to the funeral, and especially we prayed that God would give me the strength to survive the day of the funeral.

The next morning, the prayer warriors left my house. After I took my shower, I went downstairs with two of my sisters to greet Emmy's uncle's wife, who lived in the village just next to my house. The moment she laid her eyes on me, she accused me of not screaming at the top of my voice so the villagers would come out and cry with me and hold me and openly comfort me.

I was really shocked at her behavior, because I was not expecting such an outburst from her. I expected her to comfort me and tell me that, though my mother-in-law was dead, I could count on her support every single step of the way.

She made so much noise that all the village women gathered to see what was happening. My sisters took me away and instructed me to stay on the balcony of my house in order to put distance between me and the villagers.

The women followed us but couldn't get near me; however, they screamed at the tops of their voices, instructing me to start crying. One of them shouted at me to take off my slippers because my husband was dead; another also instructed me to take off my wristwatch. They said that a mourning widow should not be seen with these items.

All I heard from them simply made me mad inside. Here I was mourning the death of my husband and mother-in-law, and all these women could think of was how I should publicly display my emotions. I kept quiet and looked on from where I sat.

Later, a woman who I discovered was the chairperson of the women's meeting instructed all the screaming women to leave my compound and not return until they learned to start acting properly. She cautioned them that I had gone through enough of an ordeal and that forcing me to cry would not undo what had happened. She also reminded them that mourning came from the heart naturally and couldn't be forced. The screaming women slowly left my house. I said a silent prayer for her and openly thanked her for doing what she did.

Soon thereafter, news of these screaming women reached my parents' village and a lot of my relatives came to Emmy's village ready to protect me from similar incidents. Thankfully, that was it. Nobody bothered me, and I was able to deal with the most important issue: the funeral.

He that is our God is the God of Salvation; and unto
God the Lord belong the issues from death.

—*Psalm 68:20 (KJV)*

The Day

Finally, it was the day of the funeral. I woke up, took my shower in a daze, and dressed in my white mourning outfit.

My relatives surrounded me, and I heard them say things like "This is it", "You have to be strong", "Do not cry", "Remember the children", "All hope is not lost", etc.

I prayed earnestly for strength, because I thought I would not be able to make it through that day. For a little while I felt strong, because of all my family members. I was able to eat and actually greet some guests who came to see me.

Then I heard it. I heard the awful sound of the siren of the ambulance carrying my husband and my mother-in-law. I froze and then broke down, because that sound only meant one thing: it was really true. Emmy was truly dead, and Mama of the Universe, as I fondly called my mother-in-law, was also truly gone!

I remember being held by my mother, my sisters, and my cousins. Then everything became blank again. I looked at my mother and saw her in her own mourning outfit (my dad had died less than a year before, and my mom was still in her mourning clothes). The look she gave me when she saw me in mine is better left to the imagination. I will never forget that look; it was because I am her baby, her last of seven children. How could I be the first to be a widow? I'm sure she would never have pictured us like that together.

I was escorted to the ambulance, where I rode with my husband's body to church. He had his last church service and blessing.

After the service, I drove back with him to our village home, the home he built for us to retire to. I remember talking to him, promising him that I would take care of our three children to the best of my ability. Where I got the strength to do the talking is beyond me.

Then it was time for him and Mama to lie in state. I looked around and saw how sad people truly were, and I saw the look of pity in their faces when they looked at me. Of course it would have to be so. I had lost my husband who had just turned forty. What could be sadder than that?

When it was time for me to go pay my last respects, my people came to get me.

I stood up, very gently, and I walked to the living room where he and Mama lay. I took a good look at Mama, said a prayer for her soul, and proceeded to Emmy. I took a good look at him to convince myself it was truly him. It was.

Now I know why my people say, "Death hears no plea". If it did, Emmy would be alive today. I prayed so hard for death to release my sweetheart to me, but it never happened. Emmy just lay there like he was in a deep, peaceful sleep. I said a prayer for him, took a huge breath, and bid him farewell before I lost control of my emotions. My relatives held my hands and gently led me out.

After the burial, everything again became a blur. I got through the rest of the funeral without passing out. I was taken upstairs where my hair was shaved. This is an act of our culture performed on widows by other widows. It was done using a blade to ensure not a strand of hair was left on my head. I was cut and bled in several places. But I was a walking zombie.

Looking back, I don't know how I survived that day, but I did.

I stayed in the village five days after the burial. Each day I found myself at Emmy's graveside talking to him the way I used to, asking him what really happened, promising him to take care of his children and myself, and pleading with him to rest and not worry too much.

The day I left the village was really hard. I felt like I was leaving him behind in the village where he would be alone. But I had to leave so I could take care of the family he left behind. I went to his graveside, said my final goodbye, and left for Canada.

Come to me, all you who labor and are heavy-laden and overburdened, and I will cause you to rest. (I will ease and relieve and refresh your souls.)

—*Matthew 11:28 (AMP)*

Lessons Learned

Now I truly know the importance of having a relationship with God. Throughout this ordeal, I have hung on to God and constantly reminded him of his promises to me and my children. I have learned to embrace him, because truly in this situation, he is all I've got.

It took me some time to embrace God. When I first heard the news, I was simply mad at God. I could not pray, and I blamed him for not saving Emmy. But with time and lots of intervention from family and friends, my feelings changed. I still get mad sometimes. I still get frustrated. I still do not believe that all I have of Emmy are just memories we shared together. I still find it really difficult to believe that he would never physically walk through our door again; sometimes when I'm in the deep dark place, I can't understand why life can be so unfair.

The other lesson I have learned is about friendship and relationships. When Emmy was alive, he had quite a number of friends. After the incident, I realized that the true test of friendship comes when you are in a very difficult situation or facing very trying times. Out of all the people I would have classified as his true friends when he was alive, only a handful have truly been there for his family the way a true friend should be.

I have heard from other widows who are in similar situations that some people generally stayed away from you when you lost your spouse because they did not want to be bothered with your troubles. Others feel people generally stayed away because they did not know what to say and were uncomfortable with seeing you display emotion. Others simply feel you want to be left alone.

During the month after Emmy passed away, I had lots of visitors. The few friends I had in Ontario and well-wishers came to pay their sincere condolences every day, and my phone rang off the hook. But when I came back from Nigeria after the funeral, it seemed like people felt I was done grieving and I should move on with my life.

The visitors disappeared, and my phone hardly rang. I felt so alone—I have never felt such an overwhelming sense of loneliness like I felt when I came back from Nigeria. The truth is, before I left for Nigeria, Emmy's death seemed surreal. After the funeral, it became real, and that was when I really needed a lot of emotional support.

One thing that helped me through the loneliness was the knowledge that the Bible says we are never alone. If we put our trust in God, he will always be there for us. With this in mind, I just keep going, trusting and believing that a higher power is watching, protecting, and comforting my family in all we do.

I have come to realize that in life, when you are passing through difficult times, God will always provide help through people you never expect help to come from. It is amazing how the new relationships I have made over this short period of time have been a source of hope to me and my family.

I have also learned that I truly have to be strong, especially for my children. I realize that I am all they've got. I have to work hard to be both a mother and a father to them. I have to make sure that to the best of my ability, their needs are being met: emotionally, physically, spiritually, and financially. Though it is really hard, I try to be strong.

There are times when I feel people do not know when to tell a grieving person to be strong. I remember when I had just come back from my trip to Nigeria. My kids and I became so sick that I was unable to function. I was so tired, I lost my voice, and my boys were throwing up every hour. It was really horrible.

I called up a friend to help me out. I was so shocked when my friend chose that time to advise me that there would be times like this in the future and I needed to be strong.

I remember freezing and thinking to myself, *Be strong? Now? How is that possible when I am physically so sick? Does she not know when to advise me to be strong?*

That experience taught me a lesson: not everybody knows the meaning of the phrase "be strong", or at least when not to say the words, to someone grieving. It also made me realize the importance of having people who share similar experiences around me. They are the ones who can truly be empathetic to my situation, because they have been through what I am going through.

At this point in my life, I realize how important it is to have faith in my decisions, especially since fate has turned me into a single parent. So many people have a lot of advice to give regarding how best I should run my life. Some give advice out of genuine concern for my family's welfare, and some just feel they know exactly what my family needs and I should do things the exact way they suggest. Others have made themselves available to me if I ever need their advice.

In all, I have learned to really think long and hard about the decisions I need to make for my family. I have tuned into listening to my inner voice that people call instinct, but I refer to it as "the voice of God". I realize that whatever decisions I make will be on me, so I am really careful and consider what I think is right for my family. Then I go ahead and make the decision. Wisdom is all I pray for, like the wise King Solomon.

The greatest lesson I have learned so far is the importance of the openness between spouses, especially when it comes to their finances and planning for the unexpected. I know nobody ever wants to believe that they could face sudden death. I was once like that, but the truth is, it does happen. Death is real, and it is something everybody has to plan for. It is a good idea for couples to plan ahead. What will be the fate of the family? Will they be left in the hands of this cruel world at the mercy of people who were nice to us when we were alive and all was well? Or do we want our family to keep on going as best as they can without worrying about where their bread will come from?

Because death is no respecter of age, it is important to plan when young. I think the worst thing that can happen to grieving spouses is to see their surviving children suffer and to feel the fear of a drastic life change because there was no plan in case of the unexpected. I know a lot of people do not like to discuss this with their spouse. I also know a lot of women whose spouses choose to keep them in the dark when it comes to finances. This is a terrible mistake. The welfare of children really and truly depends on the decisions we make when we are alive, especially when children are young. I have seen and heard of a lot of children whose lives went from bright to dark because the surviving spouse just could not cope with the financial necessities of the family.

When I went to Nigeria, my brother-in-law (who is a pastor) told me about a couple who came to him. They were having a fight because the wife wanted her husband to disclose all they had to her and make her a signatory to their accounts. She was mad because she only heard from the outside what the husband had. When my brother-in-law informed the husband of the death of my husband and his age at death, he illustrated the importance of planning regardless of how young you may think you are. It made the husband do the right thing for his family.

Last but not the least, I learned that, though it is important to be strong, it is also important to let go sometimes, no matter how strong people think I should be. I find that grief is a powerful and overwhelming emotion. I know strength cannot be forced; sometimes strength comes naturally, but other times I am drawn to this deep, dark place where I become paralyzed with very depressing emotions.

One day, I feel guilty for being alive while my Emmy is not; the next day I feel thankful that I am alive to take care of our children. One day I feel happy; the next day everything makes me cry. I find it is such an emotional roller coaster. But I think, insofar as somehow I get the strength to come back up, it will always be OK. I have learned that I really do not have to be strong at all times. Contrary to what some people think, it is OK to be vulnerable sometimes.

When I feel vulnerable, I tend to gravitate towards friends who truly understand where I am at that point, and they are usually friends with similar experiences.

A wise person said to me that, in her own experience, she is also a widow. When she finds herself in the deep dark place, she pictures herself in the bottom of the ocean, and she tries to find the strength to move back up. According to her, her strength comes from the knowledge that her kids depend on her. When she remembers her kids, she finds her way out of the deep end.

I took her experience and used it as one of my "go to" tools, and it works. I have come to believe that God gives us responsibilities, like our children, and he also gives us strength to take care of our responsibilities. In times of crisis, instead of giving up, the thought of our responsibilities keeps us going.

Trust in the Lord with all thine heart; and lean not unto thine own understanding. In all thy ways acknowledge him, and he shall direct thy paths. Be not wise in thy own eyes: fear the lord, and depart from evil.

—*Proverbs 3:5–7 (KJV)*

Life as We Now Know It

My family is taking it one day at a time. It still hurts, and the crying never ends. Every day something happens that reminds me of Emmy, and I start to cry all over again: things like when parenting the children on my own becomes challenging, taking the garbage out on garbage day, fixing my car, fixing the yard, maintaining a spotless house, eating Nigerian cuisine that is home-cooked but I did not prepare, taking the kids out for a quick game of basketball to give me a break, taking the kids to activities—the list is endless.

It's funny when people say to me that I have to get over it or I really have to move on with my life because my husband is gone and is not part of my life anymore. In my heart I know it is impossible to get over it. People who advise me to move on and get over it obviously do not know what it means to lose a spouse. We were together for twelve years and married for almost ten years with three children. How can I forget that? All I do is try to learn how best to live and cope with the loss, not forget about it. Telling me to get over it is like asking me to forget about this wonderful man who has meant so much to me and my kids. My first son and my daughter are physical replicas of Emmy, and my middle son completely acts like him. When I see them every day, I see Emmy.

I am so lucky that I have children who are sensitive. They watch my mood all the time; when I am sad, they ask me, "Are you sad because of Daddy?"

When I say yes, they console me and remind me that their daddy is in heaven and is an angel now. When they feel sad, I remind them that Daddy is in heaven and will forever be with us in spirit. We have formed a dynamic in our family: when one person is down, the others will lift his or her spirits. Since we have no immediate family here, we have really learned to comfort one another.

My children have their struggles, especially my firstborn son, Nnaemeka. He is on the sensitive side and is finding it difficult to cope without his father. Sometimes at night he finds it difficult to fall asleep because he struggles with the fact that his dad will not come back home again. I pray every day that God will pull him through this ordeal.

We have a special place in our house with the picture of Jesus Christ on the cross, Emmy's picture directly underneath it, and the holy Bible and holy rosary on a small table beneath his photo. It symbolizes Jesus Christ looking down on Emmy's soul and taking good care of him wherever he is. The blessed mother Mary's picture also remembers him and takes care of his soul. I find this to be very soothing for my kids. We truly believe Emmy is in God's warm bosom, and we will meet again soon. Because Emmy's final resting place is in Nigeria and we cannot go there as often as we want, we go to the special place in our house to visit with him as many times as we want every day.

I found after the death of Emmy that celebrating the "firsts" was a big deal: the first Christmas without him, the first Easter without him, the first Mother's Day, the first Father's Day. Our tenth anniversary was the biggest hurdle of them all.

Our first Christmas without Emmy was a real struggle, but whether I dreaded it or not, Christmas came rolling by. Thankfully, the families and staff of my children's school community took it upon themselves to ensure that I and my kids had a good Christmas. The school community became our "secret Santa", and my kids had a blast opening presents. Because we got so many presents, I pulled myself together and brought out our Christmas tree so my children could have Christmas the way they are used to. This is why it is very important to have empathetic people who truly understand what it means to be brothers and sisters in Christ around you when you need them.

On New Year's Day, my first son, Nnaemeka, took his guitar and started to make up this wonderful song about his father. In his song he mostly praised Emmy for being such a wonderful father, a father he was never, ever going to forget. He went on for a good forty minutes, and I let him, because I felt it was a good way for him to let out bottled-up emotions. Towards the end of his song, he burst into tears. My heart and soul melted, but I had to be strong. I took him into my arms and consoled him.

Another day we were driving when my second son, Chidube, said, "Mom, why did God have to take Daddy so young? I am only seven, Nnaemeka just turned nine, and Adaku is just two. Why didn't he let Daddy watch us grow?"

That really touched my soul. I explained to him that God has a reason for everything. He probably wanted Daddy right now. And I also told him that we are still luckier than some people who never knew their daddy. I told him to hold on to all those memories he had with Daddy. He listened to me very quietly and nodded. I always pray to God to give me the wisdom to carry on, especially in times like that when I have to answer these questions.

My little girl, Adaku, who just turned two, still calls out for Daddy and carries his picture around. I make sure that his picture is nearby, so she holds on to the little memory she might have of him. I know that gradually this memory will fade, because she is so young, but I hope his pictures will provide a degree of closeness between them.

Valentine's Day came rolling in. Last Valentine's Day, Emmy got me this really cool two-in-one ring that could not be separated. In the box was a note:

"When two hearts are committed
To share life's ebb and flow,
As days become a lifetime,
The Bond of Love will grow"

He explained to me that it symbolized the love we had for each other and that our love would last forever and nothing would ever come between us, because our love would only get stronger by the day. He said that we would grow old together, and I remember I pretended to be an old lady. I walked and talked like a really old lady.

Emmy said to me, "Don't sell yourself short. You will be the most gorgeous old lady I'd ever laid my eyes on."

How could he not be here this year? Did he not say our love would last forever?

On Mother's Day, my children woke me up with our usual Mother's Day song. They noticed I was not in a good place, even though I tried to hide my feelings. After presenting me with the beautiful gifts they made from school, Chidube told me to stay in bed. He came back up with toasted waffles and a cup of tea. He made me breakfast in bed, just like Daddy. I was really touched at his gesture. I guess it only means one thing: yes, Emmy is gone physically, but he did leave me the best present of all, our children, to represent him at all times.

During the week of Father's Day, my children got busy at school making Father's Day presents. When I went to pick them up on Thursday prior to Father's Day weekend, my son Nnaemeka's teacher informed me that she had a talk with him. She told Nnaemeka that her father passed a while ago and that she always made presents for him. She also reminded my other son's art teacher about how making presents might be a sensitive ordeal for him.

My daughter, Adaku, made this beautiful frame for him at her day care.

Thankfully, all went well for my boys. They made their presents and hid them when they got home, just like they did when Emmy was alive. I decided to take the children to Saturday Mass that week because I wasn't sure how I was going to deal with the celebration in church on Sunday.

Come Sunday, my children woke up, and we all went to Emmy's photo. We sang him our usual Father's Day song; we prayed together; and they all placed their presents in front of his photo. At that point I couldn't help myself, and I broke down. It was a lot for me to handle. They all stopped and comforted me. They reminded me that Daddy was in heaven. I look back, and I can't thank God enough for my children.

My children decided that they want to keep their presents safe, and when they travel to Nigeria, they will take them to Emmy's resting place to show him their presents. I told them how wonderful I thought the idea was. At least now we have a new Father's Day tradition.

For our tenth anniversary, I decided to go away to a place that will mesmerize my family and me. Escaping from my situation was all I could think of, because at that point I was physically and emotionally drained. So I decided to take my children to Walt Disney World, Orlando, in the USA. It was the best decision, because my children and I were able to escape to a magical world. On 19 July 2013, the day of our anniversary, we went to Epcot Park in Disney World and experienced the most beautiful fireworks I have ever seen in my life. When Emmy was alive, he loved fireworks, so I thought it would be the best way to celebrate our anniversary. It was raining pretty heavily that night, but I was determined that not even the rain would stop us, so I got ponchos for everyone from a gift store, and we proceeded to the designated venue. The fireworks started with the illumination of the earth that was constructed so big and so beautifully. As the earth lit up and started to rotate, the fireworks began with beautiful lights shooting from the earth and filling the sky with stars, sparkles, and beautiful colors of the rainbow. Then suddenly, the earth opened up and more sparkles came out of it. It was truly mesmerizing. As I looked up in the sky, the rain hit my face, and as the sparkles continued, I could see Emmy's happy face in my mind's eye, and somehow it made the fireworks ever so special.

The Lord will keep your going out and your coming
in from this time forth and forever more.

—*Psalm 121:8 (ESV)*

In General

I believe that there is a reason for everything. I believe God brought us to Ontario for a reason, although I get a lot of questions from people about how I'm coping in this new place that we just moved to. Some even ask if I would consider moving back to Vancouver where we have lots of friends. The truth is, I am very comfortable here in Ontario; my kids adjusted quickly to the change from British Columbia to Ontario. Though my family moved for Emmy's business, personally the last year I spent in Vancouver I felt a void that I filled once I came to Ontario. I am still struggling really hard with the fact that there is a reason for the incident that claimed the life of my husband, but I believe God will, in his own time, reveal to me why his life had to end the way it did.

My boys strongly believe that Daddy is in heaven and is now their guardian angel who watches over them. They also believe that he is a saint, just like the saint that he was named after: St Marcellinus. My eldest son once asked me if Daddy died because God wants him to work as an angel for him.

I thought for a second, and I said to him, "You know what? That could be it, since he can't be alive and be an angel at the same time."

While Emmy travelled in Nigeria before the incident, he called his daughter and told her about his day. For a long time after the incident, when the phone rang, my daughter called out, "It's Daddy," and it would take me there again. She doesn't do it as frequently now as she did the first few months.

I still struggle a lot with the emotional aspect of this ordeal. I find that when I'm alone, my mind wanders off to some of the memories we shared together, and I cry like a baby. Sometimes I cry over things that are not even related to our memories.

The other thing is, I find I'm absentminded. I forget the smallest things because my mind is always wandering. In February 2013, I was driving and forgot I was driving until I heard a loud bump. I bumped into someone's car! Luckily the lady I bumped into wasn't hurt, and I ended up fixing both cars.

In March 2013, I decided to get a place to live so my kids could remain in the same school to give them some sort of stability in a world that has been nothing but one unpleasant change after another to them. The move was really stressful, but I remain thankful to those who made themselves invaluable to me and my family.

The part I did not foresee was how hard it would be to leave the house that I and Emmy rented together. When my landlord came to pick up the keys, suddenly it dawned on me that the house I was moving from was actually the last place I had seen my husband alive. I looked around, and I saw him climbing down the stairs. I went into the room he used as his office, and I saw him sitting there. It felt like I was leaving him behind. That was when I completely lost it. I cried like a baby. Fortunately, my landlord and his wife were there to console me.

Driving to my new place was not an easy task either. Because my kids were with me in the car, it took everything I had to drive "home". When I got there, I felt the emptiness all over, and I broke down in front of the kids. My second child held on to me and reminded me of the fact that Daddy was in heaven, but my first son and daughter were inconsolable. We cried so hard that we all slept on my bed that night without any dinner. At that point my head kept telling my heart to be strong for my kids, but my heart could not stop crying.

I find the toughest part of dealing with the passing away of Emmy is carrying out all the necessary formalities with society. It took me three months to realize that I had to take his name off our joint account, and doing that was no fun at all. Then I had to take his passport to the passport office to get it cancelled. I had to call Revenue Canada, Canada Pension Plan, the utility company, etc. Honestly, I do not know how I did all that, because all it did was to remind me of the finality of my situation: *I'm truly a widow.*

Performing all these tasks was really hard on me, because I did all of them on my own with no form of help either physically or emotionally from family members who are all in Nigeria. My family asked me a thousand times to move back to Nigeria for at least a year so I could heal properly; then I could decide if I wanted to move back to Canada with the children. But the thought of going to the country where this unfortunate incident happened to me and my family just gave me the shivers.

After going through the process of getting a place for me and my kids and doing all the paperwork, including filing Emmy's last tax form, I realized I really have to take care of myself. Because I buried myself in so much work so as not to think about my situation, the minute I was free, I found myself back to the deepest, darkest place of constantly questioning and wishing this whole thing never happened. On the advice of the social worker from my kids' school and the social worker I met in the hospital where I took my daughter when she was having trouble breathing because of enlarged tonsils and adenoids, I decided to join the Bereaved Families of Ontario.

The first time our group met, our first exercise was to share with the group how we lost our spouse. One lost her spouse while they were on a vacation in Germany. Another walked into her living room and found her spouse dead. Four lost their spouses to cancer, and the last one lost hers to complications from a heart condition.

After listening to all their stories, I felt there were other people going through what I was experiencing. The decision to join this group was very beneficial to me for two reasons: first, I met people with similar experiences. In the group, we all share our grief, our stories, our fears, and our worries. Because we've all lost a spouse, it is easy for us to say to each other, "I know what you mean", which I find difficult to hear from people who say it to me but who haven't lost a spouse. Secondly, I met a wonderful woman, Elizabeth Siqueira, who has turned out to be a very dear friend.

In Nigerian culture, when a family experiences loss, it is expected that the family refrains from any celebratory or merry-making event until the dead has been properly mourned for at least six months or a year, depending solely on the mourners. It shows a sign of respect to the dead and tells the world that the family is mourning. It is the same logic that applies to widows wearing solid black or solid white for six months or a year as an outward sign of grief.

When Chidube received his first holy communion in April 2013, not quite six months after the incident, he wanted a celebration just like his brother had when he received his first communion two years prior. I had to explain to Chidube that because of the unfortunate incident that happened to our family, we really could not have a party. He understood, but I could tell he felt really bad about it. I did make him a special meal and invited a very close friend of Emmy's and his family. Chidube took photos and had a special cupcake I ordered. I took him to McDonald's for dinner. Overall, he had a good and memorable day.

Therefore do not be anxious about tomorrow, for tomorrow will be anxious for itself. Sufficient for the day is its own trouble.

—*Matthew 6:34 (ESV)*

Conclusion

This ordeal is the most difficult thing I have ever faced in my life. I have heard people say that a close brush with death really changes you as a person. When I lost my father ten months before Emmy, it was a close brush, but because the family was expecting it to happen as a way of relieving him from his pain, although we were crushed, we celebrated his life.

On the other hand, because of the suddenness of the death of Emmy, its impact has been a lot for us to handle. It has changed me as a person in several ways. I have learned to "stop and smell the roses" more often now than before, because I know that our time on earth is something we have no control over. The "now" is certain; the next minute is as uncertain as pregnancy.

Spending time with my children means so much to me. Listening to them, being there for them, taking more time and interest in their schoolwork and extracurricular activities, teaching them what I know about life, and generally keeping them happy is all I live for. I don't allow little things to bother me as they did before.

Anything I don't have control over, I let go and pray that God intervenes for me or makes the problem disappear. I try to be happy. I believe what you think always finds a way of reflecting on you. I try not to dwell on the fact that too many tragedies have befallen my family; rather, I count my blessings because I have three healthy children that Emmy left me. I am healthy, we have a place to call our own, we live in a great country, and God loves us.

On one hot day in July, I took my kids to the water park. There I met a lady. After we exchanged pleasantries, she started to confide in me about some issues that had been bothering her. When she was done, I decided to share my story with her. She looked at me and said in a million years she would never have guessed that I went through an ordeal of that magnitude because, according to her, I appeared very peaceful. She said she was never again going to complain. After our conversation I left feeling happy that my prayers for divine strength had been granted to me.

Each day that passes makes me stronger to handle the challenges of life without Emmy. I do what I can and take life one day at a time. When I went to Nigeria, my eldest sister told me that sometimes when huge and overwhelming events occur in our life, it is very important to stay focused and hang on to our faith. She said that sometimes things happen to prepare us for a greater role in our life.

She reminded me of how devastating her life had been when she was forced into early retirement. She thought her life was over. She used to call me and ask me how and what she was expected to do, because she was still in her fifties and had a lot of time on her hands. Two years later she started her own catering school and is now doing so well for herself. I remember asking myself what kind of role the death of my husband would possibly prepare me for. She saw my expression and said, "Pray hard—time will tell."

As the days slowly pass by, I find new meanings to the words "be strong". Overall, these words mean to be strong for our little children. They have nobody but me. Though my days are very lonely, the nights are even worse. I try to make the children the centre of my world. I try to be there for them 100 per cent. I have also determined that "be strong" refers to an awareness that I am now a single mother.

An auntie advised me in Nigeria that my toughest ordeal would be realizing the fact that I am now like a person walking in the rain with my umbrella and suddenly someone snatches the umbrella away from me. What do I do? Do I stay in the rain, or do I try to find a solution to avoid being wet? That is where the term "be strong" comes in. I have to make sure that I stay dry notwithstanding the difficulties.

The other meaning I have attached to "be strong" is my ability to completely trust my judgment In the affairs of my family. It means to be strong enough to make decisions concerning the welfare of my children and not second-guess myself. This is where I pray daily for wisdom from God. I also attach to the meaning of "be strong" my ability to be spiritually and emotionally strong to face life head-on.

"Be strong" also means wearing the hat of Emmy in everyday situations. Prior to the incident, a lot of the financial aspects of running the family were his responsibility. Emmy was really good at checking the bills to ensure he was paying the right amount. He was also very good at paying the bills on time, taking care of the car, knowing the right mechanics, and maintaining the yard and house. The last house we sold in Vancouver was our third property. I remember how easy it was for us to sell anytime we put our house on the market. All the buyers and the Realtors commented on was how spotless and well maintained our house was. Now not only am I responsible for cooking, cleaning, homework, schoolwork tracking, and being a "taxi mom", I have to deal with all he did so well. I am finding it to be very challenging.

Because of the difficulty of playing the roles of a mother and father to my kids and just dealing with the changes that we have gone through, I decided to take some time off work and focus on myself and our kids until we get our bearings.

Sometimes people ask me, "Are you working now?"

Some even dare to ask what I do when my kids go to school. Though I find this question a little annoying, I try to ignore it and remind myself that not everybody is aware of the struggles I am going through. Like I said, because I am comfortable with my decision to stay home and focus on myself and my kids, that is really all that matters.

When Emmy was alive, he was definitely my shield. This is where the analogy of the umbrella comes in. I find that, even in situations like buying a car, salespeople give better deals to men than women! I find I have to be tough in a man's world to get similar attention that would be accorded to a man. It is very tiring.

I strongly believe that notwithstanding this nightmare, my children will be very successful in life. Growing up without a father figure will be tough on them, but we are ready to face these challenges head-on; so wherever Emmy is, he will be very proud of us.

Chidube, my second son, is very introverted in showing how he truly feels, so I tend to keep a close eye on him a lot. One day we were alone, and I asked him how he was doing. He said he was OK. I asked him if he ever misses his dad. He said that he misses his dad all the time. And I asked him how come he hardly cries. And his response shocked me. Chidube, my seven-year-old, told me that he tries not to cry because when he sees his brother Nnaemeka and me cry, he feels he should be strong for us and hold it back.

I remember stopping and taking my son into my arms. I told him that if he ever felt like crying, it was OK to cry. I told him that it was not his job to be strong for me, it is my job to be strong for him. I reminded him that in this lifetime there will definitely come a time when I will rely on him to be there for me. And when that time comes, I will be more than happy to let him be strong for me. He looked at me and smiled. At that point, I realized how much of his father's character he truly inherited.

It gives me joy to sometimes eavesdrop on my boys and hear some of the things they say about their dad. When my boys won their last basketball tournament, I heard them saying they wished Daddy was here to cheer them on because it was the type of thing he really enjoyed doing with them. When my second son, Chidube, participated in the Gymnastics Energy Boys Invitational on Saturday, 1 June 2013, he performed so well, and all I kept thinking of anytime Chidube impressed me was, *How I wish Emmy was here to see his son perform so confidently.* When my son Nnaemeka's soccer team won the tournament in the winter season, I was so proud of him, he was so proud of himself, and I just couldn't help but miss Emmy's presence.

At this point I have completely immersed myself in their active lives because it always makes me happy, and when Emmy was with us, he loved them to be active. I have hope in the strength of my family, and I know that it is well with us.

Adieu, Emmy, until we meet again.

From your loving family: Joy Uloaku Ekwommadu, Nnaemeka Denzel Ekwommadu, Chidube Charles Ekwommadu, and Adaku Annabelle Ekwommadu. You will forever be a part of our lives, and we will always love you.

Just us now ... the Lord is our strength